THE MINIATURE CODEX

A JOURNAL FOR THE INITIATED

Hello!

First off, I want to thank you for purchasing this journal.

The idea for it first came about when I was working on one of the numerous Miniatures I've made in my life. It was looking pretty good and I wanted to commemorate it in some small way.

Obviously I can do that through any of the countless websites that exist for that very purpose, but since I'm a pretty private person, I knew that those options weren't for me.

What I wanted was something that was essentially a photo album, but more than that. I realized that if I was going to take the time to actually print off pictures and collect them, I would need to have a photo-journal. One that I could use to chronicle my journey into the mini-painting world.

So here we are.

This is going to be a constantly evolving product, so if you have any notes or just want me to send you a PDF template of the entire thing, please don't hesitate to email me at: hussarpublishinggroup@gmail.com

Thank you and happy journaling!

MODEL:

PAINTS:

INSERT PHOTO HERE

NOTES:

The Miniature Codex

NOTES

MODEL:

PAINTS:

INSERT PHOTO HERE

NOTES:

The Miniature Codex

NOTES

The Miniature Codex

MODEL:

PAINTS:

NOTES:

INSERT PHOTO HERE

NOTES

MODEL:

PAINTS:

INSERT PHOTO HERE

NOTES:

NOTES

MODEL:

PAINTS:

NOTES:

INSERT PHOTO HERE

NOTES

MODEL:

PAINTS:

INSERT PHOTO HERE

NOTES:

NOTES

The Miniature Codex

MODEL:

PAINTS:

NOTES:

INSERT PHOTO HERE

NOTES

MODEL:

PAINTS:

INSERT PHOTO HERE

NOTES:

NOTES

MODEL:

PAINTS:

INSERT PHOTO HERE

NOTES:

The Miniature Codex

NOTES

MODEL:

PAINTS:

INSERT PHOTO HERE

NOTES:

The Miniature Codex

NOTES

MODEL:

PAINTS:

INSERT PHOTO HERE

NOTES:

The Miniature Codex

NOTES

MODEL:

PAINTS:

INSERT PHOTO HERE

NOTES:

NOTES

MODEL:

PAINTS:

INSERT PHOTO HERE

NOTES:

NOTES

The Miniature Codex

MODEL: _____

PAINTS: _____

_____

_____

_____

_____

_____

_____

_____

_____

_____

_____

_____

_____

_____

NOTES: _____

_____

_____

_____

_____

_____

NOTES

The Miniature Codex

MODEL:

PAINTS:

INSERT PHOTO HERE

NOTES:

NOTES

MODEL:

PAINTS:

INSERT PHOTO HERE

NOTES:

The Miniature Codex

NOTES

The Miniature Codex

MODEL:

PAINTS:

INSERT PHOTO HERE

NOTES:

NOTES

The Miniature Codex

MODEL:

PAINTS:

INSERT PHOTO HERE

NOTES:

NOTES

MODEL:

PAINTS:

INSERT PHOTO HERE

NOTES:

NOTES

MODEL:

PAINTS:

NOTES:

INSERT PHOTO HERE

NOTES

MODEL:

PAINTS:

INSERT PHOTO HERE

NOTES:

The Miniature Codex

NOTES

MODEL:

PAINTS:

INSERT PHOTO HERE

NOTES:

The Miniature Codex

NOTES

The Miniature Codex

MODEL:

PAINTS:

NOTES:

INSERT PHOTO HERE

The Miniature Codex

NOTES

MODEL:

PAINTS:

INSERT PHOTO HERE

NOTES:

NOTES

MODEL:

PAINTS:

INSERT PHOTO HERE

NOTES:

NOTES

MODEL:

PAINTS:

INSERT PHOTO HERE

NOTES:

The Miniature Codex

NOTES

MODEL:

PAINTS:

INSERT PHOTO HERE

NOTES:

The Miniature Codex

NOTES

MODEL:

PAINTS:

INSERT PHOTO HERE

NOTES:

NOTES

MODEL:

PAINTS:

INSERT PHOTO HERE

NOTES:

The Miniature Codex

NOTES

MODEL:

PAINTS:

INSERT PHOTO HERE

NOTES:

NOTES

MODEL:

PAINTS:

NOTES:

INSERT PHOTO HERE

The Miniature Codex

NOTES

MODEL:

PAINTS:

INSERT PHOTO HERE

NOTES:

The Miniature Codex

NOTES

MODEL:

PAINTS:

INSERT PHOTO HERE

NOTES:

The Miniature Codex

NOTES

The Miniature Codex

MODEL:

PAINTS:

INSERT PHOTO HERE

NOTES:

NOTES

The Miniature Codex

MODEL:

PAINTS:

INSERT PHOTO HERE

NOTES:

The Miniature Codex

NOTES

MODEL:

PAINTS:

INSERT PHOTO HERE

NOTES:

The Miniature Codex

NOTES

MODEL:

PAINTS:

INSERT PHOTO HERE

NOTES:

The Miniature Codex

NOTES

MODEL:

PAINTS:

INSERT PHOTO HERE

NOTES:

NOTES

MODEL:

PAINTS:

INSERT PHOTO HERE

NOTES:

The Miniature Codex

NOTES

The Miniature Codex

MODEL:

PAINTS:

INSERT PHOTO HERE

NOTES:

The Miniature Codex

NOTES

MODEL:

PAINTS:

INSERT PHOTO HERE

NOTES:

NOTES

MODEL:

PAINTS:

INSERT PHOTO HERE

NOTES:

The Miniature Codex

NOTES

The Miniature Codex

MODEL:

PAINTS:

INSERT PHOTO HERE

NOTES:

The Miniature Codex

NOTES

MODEL:

PAINTS:

INSERT PHOTO HERE

NOTES:

The Miniature Codex

NOTES

The Miniature Codex

MODEL:

PAINTS:

INSERT PHOTO HERE

NOTES:

The Miniature Codex

NOTES

MODEL:

PAINTS:

INSERT PHOTO HERE

NOTES:

NOTES

MODEL:

PAINTS:

INSERT PHOTO HERE

NOTES:

The Miniature Codex

NOTES

MODEL:

PAINTS:

INSERT PHOTO HERE

NOTES:

NOTES

MODEL:

PAINTS:

INSERT PHOTO HERE

NOTES:

The Miniature Codex

NOTES

MODEL:

PAINTS:

INSERT PHOTO HERE

NOTES:

NOTES

MODEL:

PAINTS:

INSERT PHOTO HERE

NOTES:

The Miniature Codex

NOTES

MODEL:

PAINTS:

INSERT PHOTO HERE

NOTES:

The Miniature Codex

NOTES

The Miniature Codex

MODEL:

PAINTS:

INSERT PHOTO HERE

NOTES:

The Miniature Codex

NOTES

The Miniature Codex

MODEL:

PAINTS:

INSERT PHOTO HERE

NOTES:

The Miniature Codex

NOTES

MODEL:

PAINTS:

INSERT PHOTO HERE

NOTES:

NOTES

Made in the USA
San Bernardino, CA
09 May 2020